HAPPY DAYS

Works by Samuel Beckett published by Grove Press

COLLECTED POEMS IN ENGLISH AND FRENCH

COLLECTED SHORTER PLAYS
(All That Fall, Act Without Words I, Act Without Words II, Krapp's Last Tape, Rough for Theatre I, Rough For Theatre II, Embers, Rough for Radio I, Rough for Radio II, Words and Music, Cascando, Play, Film, The Old Tune, Come and Go, Eh Joe, Breath, Not I, That Time, Footfalls, Ghost Trio, . . . but the clouds . . . , A Piece of Monologue, Rockaby, Ohio Impromptu, Quad, Catastrophe, Nacht and Träume, What Where)

COMPLETE SHORT PROSE: 1929–1989
(Assumption, Sedendo et Quiescendo, Text, A Case in a Thousand, First Love, The Expelled, The Calmative, The End, Texts for Nothing 1–13, From an Abandoned Work, The Image, All Strange Away, Imagination Dead Imagine, Enough, Ping, Lessness, The Lost Ones, Fizzles 1–8, Heard in the Dark 1, Heard in the Dark 2, One Evening, As the story was told, The Cliff, neither, Stirrings Still, Variations on a "Still" Point, *Faux Départs*, The Capital of the Ruins)

DISJECTA:
Miscellaneous Writings and
a Dramatic Fragment

ENDGAME AND ACT WITHOUT
WORDS

HAPPY DAYS

HOW IT IS

I CAN'T GO ON, I'LL GO ON:
A Samuel Beckett Reader

KRAPP'S LAST TAPE (All That Fall,
Embers, Act Without Words I,
Act Without Words II)

MERCIER AND CAMIER

MOLLOY

MORE PRICKS THAN KICKS
(Dante and the Lobster, Fingal,
Ding-Dong, A Wet Night,
Love and Lethe, Walking Out,
What a Misfortune,
The Smeraldina's Billet Doux,
Yellow, Draff)

MURPHY

NOHOW ON (Company,
Ill Seen Ill Said, Worstward Ho)

PROUST

STORIES AND TEXTS FOR NOTHING
(The Expelled, The Calmative,
The End, Texts for Nothing 1–13)

THREE NOVELS (Molloy,
Malone Dies, The Unnamable)

WAITING FOR GODOT

WATT

HAPPY DAYS:
Production Notebooks

WAITING FOR GODOT:
Theatrical Notebooks

SAMUEL BECKETT

HAPPY DAYS

A PLAY IN TWO ACTS

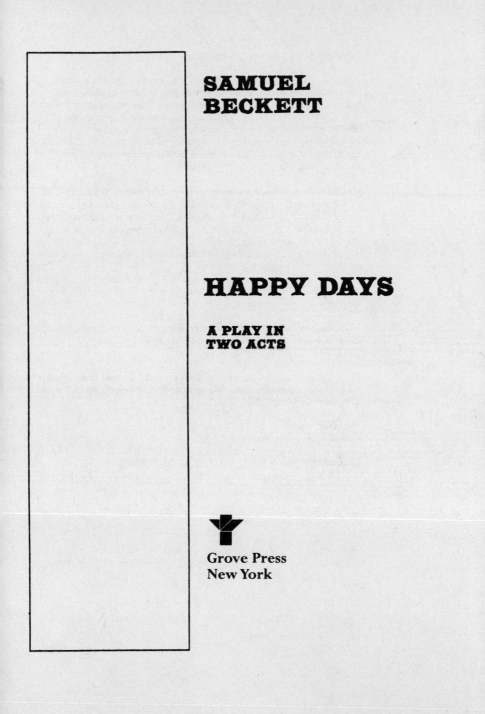

Grove Press
New York

The world première of *Happy Days* was presented by Theatre 1962 (Messrs. Richard Barr and Clinton Wilder) at the Cherry Lane Theatre, New York, on September 17, 1961, with the following cast:

WINNIE, *a woman about fifty*	Ruth White
WILLIE, *a man about sixty*	John C. Becher

Directed by Alan Schneider

Designed by William Ritman

Act I

*Expanse of scorched grass rising centre to low
mound. Gentle slopes down to front and
either side of stage. Back an abrupter fall to
stage level. Maximum of simplicity and
symmetry.*

Blazing light.

*Very pompier trompe-l'oeil backcloth to
represent unbroken plain and sky receding to
meet in far distance.*

*Imbedded up to above her waist in exact
centre of mound, WINNIE. About fifty, well
preserved, blond for preference, plump, arms
and shoulders bare, low bodice, big bosom,
pearl necklet. She is discovered sleeping, her
arms on the ground before her, her head on
her arms. Beside her on ground to her left a
capacious black bag, shopping variety, and to
her right a collapsible collapsed parasol, beak*

7

of handle emerging from sheath.

To her right and rear, lying asleep on ground, hidden by mound, WILLIE.

Long pause. A bell rings piercingly, say ten seconds, stops. She does not move. Pause. Bell more piercingly, say five seconds. She wakes. Bell stops. She raises her head, gazes front. Long pause. She straightens up, lays her hands flat on ground, throws back her head and gazes at zenith. Long pause.

WINNIE   (*gazing at zenith*). Another heavenly day. (*Pause. Head back level, eyes front, pause. She clasps hands to breast, closes eyes. Lips move in inaudible prayer, say ten seconds. Lips still. Hands remain clasped. Low.*) For Jesus Christ sake Amen. (*Eyes open, hands unclasp, return to mound. Pause. She clasps hands to breast again, closes eyes, lips move again in inaudible addendum, say five seconds. Low.*) World without end Amen. (*Eyes open, hands unclasp, return to mound. Pause.*) Begin, Winnie. (*Pause.*) Begin your day, Winnie. (*Pause. She turns to bag, rummages in it without moving it from its place, brings out toothbrush, rummages again, brings out*

*flat tube of toothpaste, turns back front,
unscrews cap of tube, lays cap on ground,
squeezes with difficulty small blob of paste on
brush, holds tube in one hand and brushes teeth
with other. She turns modestly aside and back
to her right to spit out behind mound. In this
position her eyes rest on WILLIE. She spits
out. She cranes a little further back and down.
Loud.)* Hoo-oo! *(Pause. Louder.)* Hoo-oo!
*(Pause. Tender smile as she turns back front,
lays down brush.)* Poor Willie — *(examines
tube, smile off)* — running out — *(looks for
cap)* — ah well — *(finds cap)* — can't be helped
— *(screws on cap)* — just one of those old
things — *(lays down tube)* — another of those
old things — *(turns towards bag)* — just can't
be cured — *(rummages in bag)* — cannot be
cured — *(brings out small mirror, turns back
front)* — ah yes — *(inspects teeth in mirror)* —
poor dear Willie — *(testing upper front teeth
with thumb, indistinctly)* — good Lord!
— *(pulling back upper lip to inspect gums, do.)*
— good God! — *(pulling back corner of mouth,
mouth open, do.)* — ah well — *(other corner,
do.)* — no worse — *(abandons inspection,
normal speech)* — no better, no worse — *(lays
down mirror)* — no change — *(wipes fingers on*

grass) — no pain — (*looks for toothbrush*) —
hardly any — (*takes up toothbrush*) — great
thing that — (*examines handle of brush*) —
nothing like it — (*examines handle, reads*) —
pure . . . what? — (*pause*) — what? — (*lays
down brush*) — ah yes — (*turns towards bag*)
— poor Willie — (*rummages in bag*) — no zest
— (*rummages*) — for anything — (*brings out
spectacles in case*) — no interest — (*turns back
front*) — in life — (*takes spectacles from case*)
— poor dear Willie — (*lays down case*) — sleep
for ever — (*opens spectacles*) — marvellous gift
— (*puts on spectacles*) — nothing to touch it —
(*looks for toothbrush*) — in my opinion —
(*takes up toothbrush*) — always said so —
(*examines handle of brush*) — wish I had it
— (*examines handle, reads*) — genuine . . .
pure . . . what? — (*lays down brush*) — blind
next — (*takes off spectacles*) — ah well — (*lays
down spectacles*) — seen enough — (*feels in
bodice for handkerchief*) — I suppose — (*takes
out folded handkerchief*) — by now — (*shakes
out handkerchief*) — what are those wonderful
lines — (*wipes one eye*) — woe wȯe is me —
(*wipes the other*) — to see what I see — (*looks
for spectacles*) — ah yes — (*takes up spectacles*)

— wouldn't miss it — (*starts polishing
spectacles, breathing on lenses*) — or would I?
— (*polishes*) — holy light — (*polishes*) — bob
up out of dark — (*polishes*) — blaze of hellish
light. (*Stops polishing, raises face to sky, pause,
head back level, resumes polishing, stops
polishing, cranes back to her right and down.*)
Hoo-oo! (*Pause. Tender smile as she turns
back front and resumes polishing. Smile off.*)
Marvellous gift — (*stops polishing, lays down
spectacles*) — wish I had it — (*folds handkerchief*) — ah well — (*puts handkerchief back
in bodice*) — can't complain — (*looks for
spectacles*) — no no — (*takes up spectacles*) —
mustn't complain — (*holds up spectacles, looks
through lens*) — so much to be thankful for —
(*looks through other lens*) — no pain — (*puts
on spectacles*) — hardly any — (*looks for
toothbrush*) — wonderful thing that — (*takes
up toothbrush*) — nothing like it — (*examines
handle of brush*) — slight headache sometimes
— (*examines handle, reads*) — guaranteed . . .
genuine . . . pure . . . what? — (*looks closer*)—
genuine pure . . . — (*takes handkerchief from
bodice*) — ah yes — (*shakes out handkerchief*)
— occasional mild migraine — (*starts wiping

handle of brush — it comes — (*wipes*) — then goes — (*wiping mechanically*) — ah yes — (*wiping*) — many mercies — (*wiping*) — great mercies — (*stops wiping, fixed lost gaze, brokenly*) — prayers perhaps not for naught — (*pause, do.*) — first thing — (*pause, do.*) — last thing — (*head down, resumes wiping, stops wiping, head up, calmed, wipes eyes, folds handkerchief, puts it back in bodice, examines handle of brush, reads*) — fully guaranteed... genuine pure... — (*looks closer*) — genuine pure... (*Takes off spectacles, lays them and brush down, gazes before her.*) Old things. (*Pause.*) Old eyes. (*Long pause.*) On, Winnie. (*She casts about her, sees parasol, considers it at length, takes it up and develops from sheath a handle of surprising length. Holding butt of parasol in right hand she cranes back and down to her right to hang over WILLIE.*) Hoo-oo! (*Pause.*) Willie! (*Pause.*) Wonderful gift. (*She strikes down at him with beak of parasol.*) Wish I had it. (*She strikes again. The parasol slips from her grasp and falls behind mound. It is immediately restored to her by WILLIE's invisible hand.*) Thank you, dear. (*She transfers parasol to left hand, turns*

back front and examines right palm.) Damp.
(*Returns parasol to right hand, examines left
palm.*) Ah well, no worse. (*Head up,
cheerfully.*) No better, no worse, no change.
(*Pause. Do.*) No pain. (*Cranes back to look
down at WILLIE, holding parasol by butt as
before.*) Don't go off on me again now dear
will you please, I may need you. (*Pause.*)
No hurry, no hurry, just don't curl up on me
again. (*Turns back front, lays down parasol,
examines palms together, wipes them on grass.*)
Perhaps a shade off colour just the same.
(*Turns to bag, rummages in it, brings out
revolver, holds it up, kisses it rapidly, puts it
back, rummages, brings out almost empty
bottle of red medicine, turns back front, looks
for spectacles, puts them on, reads label.*) Loss
of spirits . . . lack of keenness . . . want of
appetite . . . infants . . . children . . . adults . . .
six level . . . tablespoonfuls daily — (*head up,
smile*) — the old style! — (*smile off, head down,
reads*) — daily . . . before and after . . . meals . . .
instantaneous . . . (*looks closer*) . . . improve-
ment. (*Takes off spectacles, lays them down,
holds up bottle at arm's length to see level,
unscrews cap, swigs it off head well back, tosses*

cap and bottle away in WILLIE's direction.
Sound of breaking glass.) Ah that's better!
(Turns to bag, rummages in it, brings out
lipstick, turns back front, examines lipstick.)
Running out. (Looks for spectacles.) Ah well.
(Puts on spectacles, looks for mirror.)
Musn't complain. (Takes up mirror, starts
doing lips.) What is that wonderful line?
(Lips.) Oh fleeting joys — (lips) — oh
something lasting woe. (Lips. She is
interrupted by disturbance from WILLIE.
He is sitting up. She lowers lipstick and mirror
and cranes back and down to look at him.
Pause. Top back of WILLIE's bald head,
trickling blood, rises to view above slope,
comes to rest. WINNIE pushes up her
spectacles. Pause. His hand appears with handkerchief, spreads it on skull, disappears. Pause.
The hand appears with boater, club ribbon,
settles it on head, rakish angle, disappears.
Pause. WINNIE cranes a little further back
and down.) Slip on your drawers, dear, before
you get singed. (Pause.) No? (Pause.) Oh I
see, you still have some of that stuff left.
(Pause.) Work it well in, dear. (Pause.) Now
the other. (Pause. She turns back front, gazes

before her. Happy expression.) Oh this is going
to be another happy day! (*Pause. Happy
expression off. She pulls down spectacles and
resumes lips. WILLIE opens newspaper, hands
invisible. Tops of yellow sheets appear on
either side of his head. WINNIE finishes lips,
inspects them in mirror held a little further
away.*) Ensign crimson. (*WILLIE turns page.
WINNIE lays down lipstick and mirror, turns
towards bag.*) Pale flag.

*WILLIE turns page. WINNIE rummages in
bag, brings out small ornate brimless hat with
crumpled feather, turns back front, straightens
hat, smooths feather, raises it towards head,
arrests gesture as WILLIE reads.*

WILLIE   His Grace and Most Reverend Father in God
Dr Carolus Hunter dead in tub.

Pause.

WINNIE   (*gazing front, hat in hand, tone of fervent
reminiscence*). Charlie Hunter! (*Pause.*) I
close my eyes — (*she takes off spectacles and
does so, hat in one hand, spectacles in other,
WILLIE turns page*) — and am sitting on his
knees again, in the back garden at Borough

Green, under the horse-beech. (*Pause. She opens eyes, puts on spectacles, fiddles with hat.*) Oh the happy memories!

Pause. She raises hat towards head, arrests gesture as WILLIE reads.

WILLIE Opening for smart youth.

Pause. She raises hat towards head, arrests gesture, takes off spectacles, gazes front, hat in one hand, spectacles in other.

WINNIE My first ball! (*Long pause.*) My second ball! (*Long pause. Closes eyes.*) My first kiss! (*Pause. WILLIE turns page. WINNIE opens eyes.*) A Mr Johnson, or Johnston, or perhaps I should say John*stone*. Very bushy moustache, very tawny. (*Reverently.*) Almost ginger! (*Pause.*) Within a toolshed, though whose I cannot conceive. We had no toolshed and he most certainly had no toolshed. (*Closes eyes.*) I see the piles of pots. (*Pause.*) The tangles of bast. (*Pause.*) The shadows deepening among the rafters.

Pause. She opens eyes, puts on spectacles, raises hat towards head, arrests gesture as WILLIE reads.

WILLIE   Wanted bright boy.

> *Pause. WINNIE puts on hat hurriedly, looks
> for mirror. WILLIE turns page. WINNIE
> takes up mirror, inspects hat, lays down mirror,
> turns towards bag. Paper disappears. WINNIE
> rummages in bag, brings out magnifying-glass,
> turns back front, looks for toothbrush. Paper
> reappears, folded, and begins to fan WILLIE's
> face, hand invisible. WINNIE takes up tooth-
> brush and examines handle through glass.*

WINNIE   Fully guaranteed ... (*WILLIE stops fanning*)
... genuine pure ... (*Pause. WILLIE resumes
fanning. WINNIE looks closer, reads.*) Fully
guaranteed ... (*WILLIE stops fanning*) ...
genuine pure ... (*Pause. WILLIE resumes
fanning. WINNIE lays down glass and brush,
takes handkerchief from bodice, takes off and
polishes spectacles, puts on spectacles, looks for
glass, takes up and polishes glass, lays down
glass, looks for brush, takes up brush and wipes
handle, lays down brush, puts handkerchief
back in bodice, looks for glass, takes up glass,
looks for brush, takes up brush and examines
handle through glass.*) Fully guaranteed ...
(*WILLIE stops fanning*) ... genuine pure ...

(*pause, WILLIE resumes fanning*) . . . hog's
(*WILLIE stops fanning, pause*) . . . setae.
(*Pause. WINNIE lays down glass and brush,
paper disappears, WINNIE takes off
spectacles, lays them down, gazes front.*) Hog's
setae. (*Pause.*) That is what I find so wonderful, that not a day goes by — (*smile*) — to speak
in the old style — (*smile off*) — hardly a day,
without some addition to one's knowledge
however trifling, the addition I mean, provided
one takes the pains. (*WILLIE's hand reappears
with a postcard which he examines close to
eyes.*) And if for some strange reason no
further pains are possible, why then just close
the eyes — (*she does so*) — and wait for the
day to come — (*opens eyes*) — the happy day
to come when flesh melts at so many degrees
and the night of the moon has so many hundred
hours. (*Pause.*) That is what I find so com-
forting when I lose heart and envy the brute
beast. (*Turning towards WILLIE.*) I hope
you are taking in — (*She sees postcard, bends
lower.*) What is that you have there, Willie,
may I see? (*She reaches down with hand and
WILLIE hands her card. The hairy forearm
appears above slope, raised in gesture of giving,*

the hand open to take back, and remains in this position till card is returned. WINNIE turns back front and examines card.) Heavens what are they up to! (*She looks for spectacles, puts them on and examines card.*) *No but this is just* genuine pure filth! (*Examines card.*) Make any nice-minded person want to vomit! (*Impatience of WILLIE's fingers. She looks for glass, takes it up and examines card through glass. Long pause.*) What does that creature in the background think he's doing? (*Looks closer.*) Oh no really! (*Impatience of fingers. Last long look. She lays down glass, takes edge of card between right forefinger and thumb, averts head, takes nose between left forefinger and thumb.*) Pah! (*Drops card.*) Take it away! (*WILLIE's arm disappears. His hand reappears immediately, holding card. WINNIE takes off spectacles, lays them down, gazes before her. During what follows WILLIE continues to relish card, varying angles and distance from his eyes.*) Hog's setae. (*Puzzled expression.*) What exactly is a hog? (*Pause. Do.*) A sow of course I know, but a hog . . . (*Puzzled expression off.*) Oh well what does it matter, that is what I always say, it will come back,

that is what I find so wonderful, all comes back.
(*Pause.*) All? (*Pause.*) No, not all. (*Smile.*)
No no. (*Smile off.*) Not quite. (*Pause.*) A part.
(*Pause.*) Floats up, one fine day, out of the
blue. (*Pause.*) That is what I find so wonderful.
(*Pause. She turns towards bag. Hand and card
disappear. She makes to rummage in bag, arrests
gesture.*) No. (*She turns back front. Smile.*)
No no. (*Smile off.*) Gently Winnie. (*She
gazes front. WILLIE's hand reappears, takes
off hat, disappears with hat.*) What then?
(*Hand reappears, takes handkerchief from
skull, disappears with handkerchief. Sharply,
as to one not paying attention.*) Winnie!
(*WILLIE bows head out of sight.*) What is
the alternative? (*Pause.*) What is the al —
(*WILLIE blows nose loud and long, head and
hands invisible. She turns to look at him. Pause.
Head reappears. Pause. Hand reappears with
handkerchief, spreads it on skull, disappears.
Pause. Hand reappears with boater, settles it on
head, rakish angle, disappears. Pause.*) Would
I had let you sleep on. (*She turns back front.
Intermittent plucking at grass, head up and
down, to animate following.*) Ah yes, if only I
could bear to be alone, I mean prattle away

with not a soul to hear. (*Pause.*) Not that I
flatter myself you hear much, no Willie, God
forbid. (*Pause.*) Days perhaps when you hear
nothing. (*Pause.*) But days too when you
answer. (*Pause.*) So that I may say at all times,
even when you do not answer and perhaps hear
nothing, Something of this is being heard, I am
not merely talking to myself, that is in the
wilderness, a thing I could never bear to do —
for any length of time. (*Pause.*) That is what
enables me to go on, go on talking that is.
(*Pause.*) Whereas if you were to die — (*smile*)
— to speak in the old style — (*smile off*) — or go
away and leave me, then what would I do, what
could I do, all day long, I mean between the
bell for waking and the bell for sleep? (*Pause.*)
Simply gaze before me with compressed lips.
(*Long pause while she does so. No more
plucking.*) Not another word as long as I drew
breath, nothing to break the silence of this
place. (*Pause.*) Save possibly, now and then,
every now and then, a sigh into my looking-
glass. (*Pause.*) Or a brief . . . gale of laughter,
should I happen to see the old joke again.
(*Pause. Smile appears, broadens and seems
about to culminate in laugh when suddenly*

replaced by expression of anxiety.) My hair!
(*Pause.*) Did I brush and comb my hair?
(*Pause.*) I may have done. (*Pause.*) Normally
I do. (*Pause.*) There is so little one *can* do.
(*Pause.*) One does it all. (*Pause.*) All one can.
(*Pause.*) Tis only human. (*Pause.*) Human
nature. (*She begins to inspect mound, looks
up.*) Human weakness. (*She resumes inspection
of mound, looks up.*) Natural weakness. (*She
resumes inspection of mound.*) I see no comb.
(*Inspects.*) Nor any hairbrush. (*Looks up.
Puzzled expression. She turns to bag, rummages
in it.*) The comb is here. (*Back front. Puzzled
expression. Back to bag. Rummages.*) The
brush is here. (*Back front. Puzzled expression.*)
Perhaps I put them back, after use. (*Pause.
Do.*) But normally I do not put things back,
after use, no, I leave them lying about and put
them back all together, at the end of the day.
(*Smile.*) To speak in the old style. (*Pause.*)
The sweet old style. (*Smile off.*) And yet
. . . I seem . . . to remember . . . (*Suddenly
careless.*) Oh well, what does it matter, that
is what I always say, I shall simply brush and
comb them later on, purely and simply, I have
the whole — (*Pause. Puzzled.*) Them? (*Pause.*)

Or it? (*Pause.*) *Brush and comb it?* (*Pause.*)
Sounds improper somehow. (*Pause. Turning a
little towards WILLIE.*) What would you say,
Willie? (*Pause. Turning a little further.*) What
would you say, Willie, speaking of your hair,
them or it? (*Pause.*) The hair on your head, I
mean. (*Pause. Turning a little further.*) The
hair on your head, Willie, what would you say
speaking of the hair on your head, them or it?

Long pause.

WILLIE   It.

WINNIE   (*turning back front, joyful*). Oh you are going
to talk to me today, this is going to be a happy
day! (*Pause. Joy off.*) Another happy day.
(*Pause.*) Ah well, where was I, my hair, yes,
later on, I shall be thankful for it later on.
(*Pause.*) I have my — (*raises hands to hat*) — yes,
on, my hat on — (*lowers hands*) — I cannot take
it off now. (*Pause.*) To think there are times
one cannot take off one's hat, not if one's life
were at stake. Times one cannot put it on, times
one cannot take it off. (*Pause.*) How often I
have said, Put on your hat now, Winnie, there
is nothing else for it, take off your hat now,
Winnie, like a good girl, it will do you good,

and did not. (*Pause.*) Could not. (*Pause. She raises hand, frees a strand of hair from under hat, draws it towards eye, squints at it, lets it go, hand down.*) Golden you called it, that day, when the last guest was gone — (*hand up in gesture of raising a glass*) — to your golden . . . may it never . . . (*voice breaks*) . . . may it never . . . (*Hand down. Head down. Pause. Low.*) That day. (*Pause. Do.*) What day? (*Pause. Head up. Normal voice.*) What now? (*Pause.*) Words fail, there are times when even they fail. (*Turning a little towards WILLIE.*) Is that not so, Willie? (*Pause. Turning a little further.*) Is not that so, Willie, that even words fail, at times? (*Pause. Back front.*) What is one to do then, until they come again? Brush and comb the hair, if it has not been done, or if there is some doubt, trim the nails if they are in need of trimming, these things tide one over. (*Pause.*) That is what I mean. (*Pause.*) That is all I mean. (*Pause.*) That is what I find so wonderful, that not a day goes by — (*smile*) — to speak in the old style — (*smile off*) — without some blessing — (*WILLIE collapses behind slope, his head disappears, WINNIE turns towards event*) — in disguise. (*She cranes back and down.*) Go back into your hole now, Willie, you've exposed yourself enough. (*Pause.*) Do as I say, Willie, don't lie sprawling there in this hellish sun, go back into your hole. (*Pause.*) Go on now, Willie. (*WILLIE invisible starts crawling left towards hole.*) That's the man. (*She follows his progress with her eyes.*) Not head first, stupid, how are you going to turn? (*Pause.*) That's it . . . right round . . . now . . . back in. (*Pause.*) Oh I know it is not easy, dear, crawling backwards, but it is rewarding in the end. (*Pause.*) You have left your vaseline behind. (*She watches as he crawls back for vaseline.*) The lid! (*She watches as he crawls back towards hole. Irritated.*) Not head first, I tell you! (*Pause.*) More to the right. (*Pause.*) The *right*, I said. (*Pause. Irritated.*) Keep your tail down, can't you! (*Pause.*) Now. (*Pause.*) There! (*All these directions loud. Now in her normal voice, still turned towards him.*) Can you hear me? (*Pause.*) I beseech you, Willie, just yes or no, can you hear me, just yes or nothing.

Pause.

WILLIE   Yes.

WINNIE (*turning front, same voice*). And now?

WILLIE (*irritated*). Yes.

WINNIE (*less loud*). And now?

WILLIE (*more irritated*). Yes.

WINNIE (*still less loud*). And now? (*A little louder.*) And now?

WILLIE (*violently*). Yes!

WINNIE (*same voice*). Fear no more the heat o' the sun. (*Pause.*) Did you hear that?

WILLIE (*irritated*). Yes.

WINNIE (*same voice*). What? (*Pause.*) What?

WILLIE (*more irritated*). Fear no more.

Pause.

WINNIE (*same voice*). No more what? (*Pause.*) Fear no more what?

WILLIE (*violently*). Fear no more!

WINNIE (*normal voice, gabbled*). Bless you Willie I do appreciate your goodness I know what an effort it costs you, now you may relax I shall not trouble you again unless I am obliged to, by

that I mean unless I come to the end of my own
resources which is most unlikely, just to know
that in theory you can hear me even though in
fact you don't is all I need, just to feel you
there within earshot and conceivably on the
qui vive is all I ask, not to say anything I would
not wish you to hear or liable to cause you
pain, not to be just babbling away on
trust as it is were not knowing and something
gnawing at me. (*Pause for breath.*) Doubt.
(*Places index and second finger on heart area,
moves them about, brings them to rest.*) Here.
(*Moves them slightly.*) Abouts. (*Hand away.*)
Oh no doubt the time will come when before
I can utter a word I must make sure you heard
the one that went before and then no doubt
another come another time when I must learn
to talk to myself a thing I could never bear to
do such wilderness. (*Pause.*) Or gaze before me
with compressed lips. (*She does so.*) All day
long. (*Gaze and lips again.*) No. (*Smile.*) No
no. (*Smile off.*) There is of course the bag.
(*Turns towards it.*) There will always be the
bag. (*Back front.*) Yes, I suppose so. (*Pause.*)
Even when you are gone, Willie. (*She turns a
little towards him.*) You *are* going, Willie, aren't

you? (*Pause. Louder.*) You *will* be going
soon, Willie, won't you? (*Pause. Louder.*)
Willie! (*Pause. She cranes back and down to
look at him.*) So you have taken off your
straw, that is wise. (*Pause.*) You do look snug,
I must say, with your chin on your hands and
the old blue eyes like saucers in the shadows.
(*Pause.*) Can you see me from there I wonder,
I still wonder. (*Pause.*) No? (*Back front.*) Oh
I know it does not follow when two are
gathered together — (*faltering*) — in this way
— (*normal*) — that because one sees the other
the other sees the one, life has taught me that
. . . too. (*Pause.*) Yes, life I suppose, there is no
other word. (*She turns a little towards him.*)
Could you see me, Willie, do you think, from
where you are, if you were to raise your eyes
in my direction? (*Turns a little further.*) Lift
up your eyes to me, Willie, and tell me can you
see me, do that for me, I'll lean back as far as I
can. (*Does so. Pause.*) No? (*Pause.*) Well
never mind. (*Turns back painfully front.*) The
earth is very tight today, can it be I have put
on flesh, I trust not. (*Pause. Absently, eyes
lowered.*) The great heat possibly. (*Starts to
pat and stroke ground.*) All things expanding,

some more than others. (*Pause. Patting and
stroking.*) Some less. (*Pause. Do.*) Oh I can
well imagine what is passing through your mind,
it is not enough to have to listen to the woman,
now I must look at her as well. (*Pause. Do.*)
Well it is very understandable. (*Pause. Do.*)
Most understandable. (*Pause. Do.*) One does
not appear to be asking a great deal, indeed at
times it would seem hardly possible — (*voice
breaks, falls to a murmur*) — to ask less — of a
fellow-creature — to put it mildly — whereas
actually — when you think about it — look into
your heart — see the other — what he needs —
peace — to be left in peace — then perhaps the
moon — all this time — asking for the moon.
(*Pause. Stroking hand suddenly still. Lively.*)
Oh I say, what have we here? (*Bending head to
ground, incredulous.*) Looks like life of some
kind! (*Looks for spectacles, puts them on,
bends closer. Pause.*) An emmet! (*Recoils.
Shrill.*) Willie, an emmet, a live emmet!
(*Seizes magnifying-glass, bends to ground
again, inspects through glass.*) Where's it gone?
(*Inspects.*) Ah! (*Follows its progress through
grass.*) Has like a little white ball in its arms.
(*Follows progress. Hand still. Pause.*) It's gone

in. (*Continues a moment to gaze at spot through glass, then slowly straightens up, lays down glass, takes off spectacles and gazes before her, spectacles in hand. Finally.*) Like a little white ball.

Long pause. Gesture to lay down spectacles.

WILLIE   Eggs.

WINNIE   (*arresting gesture*). What?

Pause.

WILLIE   Eggs. (*Pause. Gesture to lay down glasses.*) Formication.

WINNIE   (*arresting gesture*). What?

Pause.

WILLIE   Formication.

Pause. She lays down spectacles, gazes before her. Finally.

WINNIE   (*murmur*). God. (*Pause. WILLIE laughs quietly. After a moment she joins in. They laugh quietly together. WILLIE stops. She laughs on a moment alone. WILLIE joins in. They laugh together. She stops. WILLIE laughs on a moment alone. He stops. Pause.*

Normal voice.) Ah well what a joy in any case
to hear you laugh again, Willie, I was
convinced I never would, you never would.
(*Pause.*) I suppose some people might think us
a trifle irreverent, but I doubt it. (*Pause.*) How
can one better magnify the Almighty than by
sniggering with him at his little jokes,
particularly the poorer ones? (*Pause.*) I think
you would back me up there, Willie. (*Pause.*)
Or were we perhaps diverted by two quite
different things? (*Pause.*) Oh well, what does
it matter, that is what I always say, so long
as one . . . you know . . . what is that wonderful
line . . . laughing wild . . . something something
laughing wild amid severest woe. (*Pause.*) And
now? (*Long pause.*) Was I lovable once,
Willie? (*Pause.*) Was I ever lovable? (*Pause.*)
Do not misunderstand my question, I am not
asking you if you loved me, we know all about
that, I am asking you if you found me lovable —
at one stage. (*Pause.*) No? (*Pause.*) You can't?
(*Pause.*) Well I admit it is a teaser. And you
have done more than your bit already, for the
time being, just lie back now and relax, I shall
not trouble you again unless I am compelled to,
just to know you are there within hearing and

conceivably on the semi-alert is . . . er . . .
paradise enow. (*Pause.*) The day is now well
advanced. (*Smile.*) To speak in the old style.
(*Smile off.*) And yet it is perhaps a little soon
for my song. (*Pause.*) To sing too soon is a
great mistake, I find. (*Turning towards bag.*)
There is of course the bag. (*Looking at bag.*)
The bag. (*Back front.*) Could I enumerate
its contents? (*Pause.*) No. (*Pause.*) Could
I, if some kind person were to come along and
ask, What all have you got in that big black bag,
Winnie? give an exhaustive answer? (*Pause.*)
No. (*Pause.*) The depths in particular, who
knows what treasures. (*Pause.*) What comforts.
(*Turns to look at bag.*) Yes, there is the bag.
(*Back front.*) But something tells me, Do not
overdo the bag, Winnie, make use of it of
course, let it help you . . . along, when stuck,
by all means, but cast your mind forward,
something tells me, cast your mind forward,
Winnie, to the time when words must fail —
(*she closes eyes, pause, opens eyes*) — and do
not overdo the bag. (*Pause. She turns to look
at bag.*) Perhaps just one quick dip. (*She turns
back front, closes eyes, throws out left arm,
plunges hand in bag and brings out revolver.*

Disgusted.) You again! (*She opens eyes, brings
revolver front and contemplates it. She weighs
it in her palm.*) You'd think the weight of this
thing would bring it down among the . . . last
rounds. But no. It doesn't. Ever uppermost,
like Browning. (*Pause.*) Brownie . . . (*Turning
a little towards WILLIE.*) Remember
Brownie, Willie? (*Pause.*) Remember how
you used to keep on at me to take it away from
you? Take it away, Winnie, take it away,
before I put myself out of my misery. (*Back
front. Derisive.*) *Your* misery! (*To revolver.*)
Oh I suppose it's a comfort to know you're
there, but I'm tired of you. (*Pause.*) I'll leave
you out, that's what I'll do. (*She lays revolver
on ground to her right.*) There, that's your
home from this day out. (*Smile.*) The old style!
(*Smile off.*) And now? (*Long pause.*) Is
gravity what it was, Willie, I fancy not.
(*Pause.*) Yes, the feeling more and more that
if I were not held — (*gesture*) — in this way,
I would simply float up into the blue. (*Pause.*)
And that perhaps some day the earth will yield
and let me go, the pull is so great, yes, crack all
round me and let me out. (*Pause.*) Don't you
ever have that feeling, Willie, of being sucked

up? (*Pause.*) Don't you have to cling on
sometimes, Willie? (*Pause. She turns a little
towards him.*) Willie.

Pause.

WILLIE   *Sucked* up?

WINNIE   Yes love, up into the blue, like gossamer.
(*Pause.*) No? (*Pause.*) You don't? (*Pause.*)
Ah well, natural laws, natural laws, I suppose
it's like everything else, it all depends on the
creature you happen to be. All I can say is for
my part is that for me they are not what they
were when I was young and ... foolish and
... (*faltering, head down*) ... beautiful ...
possibly ... lovely ... in a way ... to look at.
(*Pause. Head up.*) Forgive me, Willie, sorrow
keeps breaking in. (*Normal voice.*) Ah well
what a joy in any case to know you are there,
as usual, and perhaps awake, and perhaps taking
all this in, some of all this, what a happy day
for me ... it will have been. (*Pause.*) So far.
(*Pause.*) What a blessing nothing grows,
imagine if all this stuff were to start growing.
(*Pause.*) Imagine. (*Pause.*) Ah yes, great
mercies. (*Long pause.*) I can say no more.
(*Pause.*) For the moment. (*Pause. Turns to*

look at bag. Back front. Smile.) No no. (*Smile
off. Looks at parasol.*)I suppose I might—(*takes
up parasol*) — yes, I suppose I might . . . hoist
this thing now. (*Begins to unfurl it. Following
punctuated by mechanical difficulties over-
come.*) One keeps putting off — putting up —
for fear of putting up — too soon — and the day
goes by — quite by — without one's having put
up — at all. (*Parasol now fully open. Turned
to her right she twirls it idly this way and that.*)
Ah yes, so little to say, so little to do, and the
fear so great, certain days, of finding oneself
. . . left, with hours still to run, before the bell
for sleep, and nothing more to say, nothing
more to do, that the days go by, certain days
go by, quite by, the bell goes, and little or
nothing said, little or nothing done. (*Raising
parasol.*) That is the danger. (*Turning front.*)
To be guarded against. (*She gazes front,
holding up parasol with right hand. Maximum
pause.*) I used to perspire freely. (*Pause.*) Now
hardly at all. (*Pause.*) The heat is much greater.
(*Pause.*) The perspiration much less. (*Pause.*)
That is what I find so wonderful. (*Pause.*)
The way man adapts himself. (*Pause.*) To
changing conditions. (*She transfers parasol to*

left hand. Long pause.) Holding up wearies the arm. (*Pause.*) Not if one is going along. (*Pause.*) Only if one is at rest. (*Pause.*) That is a curious observation. (*Pause.*) I hope you heard that, Willie, I should be grieved to think you had not heard that. (*She takes parasol in both hands. Long pause.*) I am weary, holding it up, and I cannot put it down. (*Pause.*) I am worse off with it up than with it down, and I cannot put it down. (*Pause.*) Reason says, Put it down, Winnie, it is not helping you, put the thing down and get on with something else. (*Pause.*) I cannot. (*Pause.*) I cannot move. (*Pause.*) No, something must happen, in the world, take place, some change, I cannot, if I am to move again. (*Pause.*) Willie. (*Mildly.*) Help. (*Pause.*) No? (*Pause.*) Bid me put this thing down, Willie, I would obey you instantly, as I have always done, honoured and obeyed. (*Pause.*) Please, Willie. (*Mildly.*) For pity's sake. (*Pause.*) No? (*Pause.*) You can't? (*Pause.*) Well I don't blame you, no, it would ill become me, who cannot move, to blame my Willie because he cannot speak. (*Pause.*) Fortunately I am in tongue again. (*Pause.*) That is what I find so wonderful, my two

lamps, when one goes out the other burns
brighter. (*Pause.*) Oh yes, great mercies.
(*Maximum pause. The parasol goes on fire.
Smoke, flames if feasible. She sniffs, looks up,
throws parasol to her right behind mound,
cranes back to watch it burning. Pause.*) Ah
earth you old extinguisher. (*Back front.*)
I presume this has occurred before, though I
cannot recall it. (*Pause.*) Can you, Willie?
(*Turns a little towards him.*) Can you recall
this having occurred before? (*Pause. Cranes
back to look at him.*) Do you know what has
occurred, Willie? (*Pause.*) Have you gone off
on me again? (*Pause.*) I do not ask if you are
alive to all that is going on, I merely ask if you
have not gone off on me again. (*Pause.*) Your
eyes appear to be closed, but that has no
particular significance we know. (*Pause.*)
Raise a finger, dear, will you please, if you are
not quite senseless. (*Pause.*) Do that for me,
Willie please, just the little finger, if you are
still conscious. (*Pause. Joyful.*) Oh all five, you
are a darling today, now I may continue with
an easy mind. (*Back front.*) Yes, what ever
occurred that did not occur before and yet . . .
I wonder, yes, I confess I wonder. (*Pause.*)

With the sun blazing so much fiercer down,
and hourly fiercer, is it not natural things
should go on fire never known to do so, in this
way I mean, spontaneous like. (*Pause.*) Shall I
myself not melt perhaps in the end, or burn, oh
I do not mean necessarily burst into flames, no,
just little by little be charred to a black cinder,
all this — (*ample gesture of arms*) — visible
flesh. (*Pause.*) On the other hand, did I ever
know a temperate time? (*Pause.*) No. (*Pause.*)
I speak of temperate times and torrid times,
they are empty words. (*Pause.*) I speak of
when I was not yet caught — in this way —
and had my legs and had the use of my legs,
and could seek out a shady place, like you,
when I was tired of the sun, or a sunny place
when I was tired of the shade, like you, and
they are all empty words. (*Pause.*) It is no
hotter today than yesterday, it will be no hotter
tomorrow than today, how could it, and so on
back into the far past, forward into the far
future. (*Pause.*) And should one day the earth
cover my breasts, then I shall never have seen
my breasts, no one ever seen my breasts.
(*Pause.*) I hope you caught something of that,
Willie, I should be sorry to think you had

caught nothing of all that, it is not every day I rise to such heights. (*Pause.*) Yes, something seems to have occurred, something has seemed to occur, and nothing has occurred, nothing at all, you are quite right, Willie. (*Pause.*) The sunshade will be there again tomorrow, beside me on this mound, to help me through the day. (*Pause. She takes up mirror.*) I take up this little glass, I shiver it on a stone — (*does so*) — I throw it away — (*does so far behind her*) — it will be in the bag again tomorrow, without a scratch, to help me through the day. (*Pause.*) No, one can do nothing. (*Pause.*) That is what I find so wonderful, the way things . . . (*voice breaks, head down*) . . . things . . . so wonderful. (*Long pause, head down. Finally turns, still bowed, to bag, brings out unidentifiable odds and ends, stuffs them back, fumbles deeper, brings out finally musical-box, winds it up, turns it on, listens for a moment holding it in both hands, huddled over it, turns back front, straightens up and listens to tune, holding box to breast with both hands. It plays the Waltz Duet "I love you so" from* The Merry Widow. *Gradually happy expression. She sways to the rhythm. Music stops. Pause.*

*Brief burst of hoarse song without words —
musical-box tune — from WILLIE. Increase
of happy expression. She lays down box.*) Oh
this will have been a happy day! (*She claps
hands.*) Again, Willie, again! (*Claps.*) Encore,
Willie, please! (*Pause. Happy expression off.*)
No? You won't do that for me? (*Pause.*) Well
it is very understandable, very understandable.
One cannot sing just to please someone,
however much one loves them, no, song
must come from the heart, that is what I
always say, pour out from the inmost, like a
thrush. (*Pause.*) How often I have said, in evil
hours, Sing now, Winnie, sing your song, there
is nothing else for it, and did not. (*Pause.*)
Could not. (*Pause.*) No, like the thrush, or
the bird of dawning, with no thought of
benefit, to oneself or anyone else. (*Pause.*) And
now? (*Long pause. Low.*) Strange feeling.
(*Pause. Do.*) Strange feeling that someone is
looking at me. I am clear, then dim, then gone,
then dim again, then clear again, and so on,
back and forth, in and out of someone's eye.
(*Pause. Do.*) Strange? (*Pause. Do.*) No, here
all is strange. (*Pause. Normal voice.*)
Something says, Stop talking now, Winnie, for

a minute, don't squander all your words for the
day, stop talking and do something for a
change, will you? (*She raises hands and holds
them open before her eyes. Apostrophic.*) Do
something! (*She closes hands.*) What claws!
(*She turns to bag, rummages in it, brings out
finally a nailfile, turns back front and begins to
file nails. Files for a time in silence, then the
following punctuated by filing.*) There floats
up — into my thoughts — a Mr Shower — a Mr
and perhaps a Mrs Shower — no — they are
holding hands — his fiancée then more likely —
or just some — loved one. (*Looks closer at
nails.*) Very brittle today. (*Resumes filing.*)
Shower — Shower — does the name mean
anything — to you, Willie — evoke any reality,
I mean — for you, Willie — don't answer if you
don't — feel up to it — you have done more —
than your bit — already — Shower — Shower.
(*Inspects filed nails.*) Bit more like it. (*Raises
head, gazes front.*) Keep yourself nice, Winnie,
that's what I always say, come what may, keep
yourself nice. (*Pause. Resumes filing.*) Yes —
Shower — Shower — (*stops filing, raises head,
gazes front, pause*) — or Cooker, perhaps I
should say Cooker. (*Turning a little towards*

WILLIE.) Cooker, Willie, does Cooker strike
a chord? (*Pause. Turns a little further.
Louder.*) Cooker, Willie, does Cooker ring a
bell, the name Cooker? (*Pause. She cranes back
to look at him. Pause.*) Oh really! (*Pause.*)
Have you no handkerchief, darling? (*Pause.*)
Have you no delicacy? (*Pause.*) Oh, Willie,
you're not eating it! Spit it out, dear, spit it
out! (*Pause. Back front.*) Ah well, I suppose
it's only natural. (*Break in voice.*) Human.
(*Pause. Do.*) What *is* one to do? (*Head down.
Do.*) All day long. (*Pause. Do.*) Day after day.
(*Pause. Head up. Smile. Calm.*) The old style!
(*Smile off. Resumes nails.*) No, done him.
(*Passes on to next.*) Should have put on my
glasses. (*Pause.*) Too late now. (*Finishes
left hand, inspects it.*) Bit more human.
(*Starts right hand. Following punctuated
as before.*) Well anyway — this man
Shower — or Cooker — no matter — and
the woman — hand in hand — in the other hands
bags — kind of big brown grips — standing there
gaping at me — and at last this man Shower —
or Cooker — ends in er anyway — stake my life
on that — What's she doing? he says — What's
the idea? he says — stuck up to her diddies in

the bleeding ground — coarse fellow — What
does it mean? he says — What's it meant to
mean? — and so on — lot more stuff like that
— usual drivel — Do you hear me? he says —
I do, she says, God help me — What do you
mean, he says, God help you? (*Stops filing,
raises head, gazes front.*) And you, she says,
what's the idea of you, she says, what are you
meant to mean? It is because you're still on
your two flat feet, with your old ditty full of
tinned muck and changes of underwear,
dragging me up and down this fornicating
wilderness, coarse creature, fit mate — (*with
sudden violence*) — let go of my hand and drop
for God's sake, she says, drop! (*Pause. Resumes
filing.*) Why doesn't he dig her out? he says —
referring to you, my dear — What good is she
to him like that? — What good is he to her like
that? — and so on — usual tosh — Good! she
says, have a heart for God's sake — Dig her out,
he says, dig her out, no sense in her like that —
Dig her out with what? she says — I'd dig her
out with my bare hands, he says — must have
been man and — wife. (*Files in silence.*) Next
thing they're away — hand in hand — and the
bags — dim — then gone — last human kind —

to stray this way. (*Finishes right hand, inspects it, lays down file, gazes front.*) Strange thing, time like this, drift up into the mind. (*Pause.*) Strange? (*Pause.*) No, here all is strange. (*Pause.*) Thankful for it in any case. (*Voice breaks.*) Most thankful. (*Head down. Pause. Head up. Calm.*) Bow and raise the head, bow and raise, always that. (*Pause.*) And now? (*Long pause. Starts putting things back in bag, toothbrush last. This operation, interrupted by pauses as indicated, punctuates following.*) It is perhaps a little soon — to make ready — for the night — (*stops tidying, head up, smile*) — the old style! — (*smile off, resumes tidying*) — and yet I do — make ready for the night — feeling it at hand — the bell for sleep — saying to myself — Winnie — it will not be long now, Winnie — until the bell for sleep. (*Stops tidying, head up.*) Sometimes I am wrong. (*Smile.*) But not often. (*Smile off.*) Sometimes all is over, for the day, all done, all said, all ready for the night, and the day not over, far from over, the night not ready, far, far from ready. (*Smile.*) But not often. (*Smile off.*) Yes, the bell for sleep, when I feel it at hand, and so make ready for the night — (*gesture*) — in this

way, sometimes I am wrong — (*smile*) — but
not often. (*Smile off. Resumes tidying.*) I used
to think — I say I used to think — that all these
things — put back into the bag — if too soon —
put back too soon — could be taken out again —
if necessary — if needed — and so on —
indefinitely — back into the bag — back out
of the bag — until the bell — went. (*Stops
tidying, head up, smile.*) But no. (*Smile
broader.*) No no. (*Smile off. Resumes
tidying.*) I suppose this — might seem
strange — this — what shall I say — this
what I have said — yes — (*she takes up
revolver*) — strange — (*she turns to put
revolver in bag*) — were it not — (*about to put
revolver in bag she arrests gesture and turns
back front*) — were it not — (*she lays down
revolver to her right, stops tidying, head up*) —
that all seems strange. (*Pause.*) Most strange.
(*Pause.*) Never any change. (*Pause.*) And more
and more strange. (*Pause. She bends to mound
again, takes up last object, i.e. toothbrush, and
turns to put it in bag when her attention is
drawn to disturbance from WILLIE. She
cranes back and to her right to see. Pause.*)
Weary of your hole, dear? (*Pause.*) Well I

can understand that. (*Pause.*) Don't forget
your straw. (*Pause.*) Not the crawler you were,
poor darling. (*Pause.*) No, not the crawler
I gave my heart to. (*Pause.*) The hands and
knees, love, try the hands and knees. (*Pause.*)
The knees! The knees! (*Pause.*) What a curse,
mobility! (*She follows with eyes his progress
towards her behind mound, i.e. towards place
he occupied at beginning of act.*) Another foot,
Willie, and you're home. (*Pause as she observes
last foot.*) Ah! (*Turns back front laboriously,
rubs neck.*) Crick in my neck admiring you.
(*Rubs neck.*) But it's worth it, well worth it.
(*Turning slightly towards him.*) Do you know
what I dream sometimes? (*Pause.*) What I
dream sometimes, Willie. (*Pause.*) That you'll
come round and live this side where I could see
you. (*Pause. Back front.*) I'd be a different
woman. (*Pause.*) Unrecognizable. (*Turning
slightly towards him.*) Or just now and then,
come round this side just every now and then
and let me feast on you. (*Back front.*) But you
can't, I know. (*Head down.*) I know. (*Pause.
Head up.*) Well anyway — (*looks at toothbrush in her hand*) — can't be long now —
(*looks at brush*) — until the bell. (*Top back of*

WILLIE's head appears above slope. WINNIE looks closer at brush.) Fully guaranteed ... (*head up*) ... what's this it was? (*WILLIE's hand appears with handkerchief, spreads it on skull, disappears.*) Genuine pure ... fully guaranteed ... (*WILLIE's hand appears with boater, settles it on head, rakish angle, disappears*) ... genuine pure ... ah! hog's setae. (*Pause.*) What is a hog exactly? (*Pause. Turns slightly towards WILLIE.*) What exactly is a hog, Willie, do you know, I can't remember. (*Pause. Turning a little further, pleading.*) What *is* a hog, Willie, please!

Pause.

WILLIE   Castrated male swine. (*Happy expression appears on WINNIE's face.*) Reared for slaughter.

Happy expression increases. WILLIE opens newspaper, hands invisible. Tops of yellow sheets appear on either side of his head. WINNIE gazes before her with happy expression.

WINNIE   Oh this *is* a happy day! This will have been

another happy day! (*Pause.*) After all.
(*Pause.*) So far.

*Pause. Happy expression off. WILLIE
turns page. Pause. He turns another page.
Pause.*

WILLIE   Opening for smart youth.

*Pause. WINNIE takes off hat, turns to put it
in bag, arrests gesture, turns back front. Smile.*

WINNIE   No. (*Smile broader.*) No no. (*Smile off. Puts
on hat again, gazes front, pause.*) And now?
(*Pause.*) Sing. (*Pause.*) Sing your song,
Winnie. (*Pause.*) No? (*Pause.*) Then pray.
(*Pause.*) Pray your prayer, Winnie.

Pause. WILLIE turns page. Pause.

WILLIE   Wanted bright boy.

*Pause. WINNIE gazes before her. WILLIE
turns page. Pause. Newspaper disappears.
Long pause.*

WINNIE   Pray your old prayer, Winnie.

Long pause.

CURTAIN

Act II

Scene *as before.*

WINNIE imbedded up to neck, hat on head, eyes closed. Her head, which she can no longer turn, nor bow, nor raise, faces front motionless throughout act. Movements of eyes as indicated.

Bag and parasol as before. Revolver conspicuous to her right on mound.

Long pause.

Bell rings loudly. She opens eyes at once. Bell stops. She gazes front. Long pause.

WINNIE   Hail, holy light. (*Long pause. She closes her eyes. Bell rings loudly. She opens eyes at once. Bell stops. She gazes front. Long smile. Smile off. Long pause.*) Someone is looking at me still. (*Pause.*) Caring for me still. (*Pause.*) That is what I find so wonderful. (*Pause.*)

49

Eyes on my eyes. (*Pause.*) What is that un-
forgettable line? (*Pause. Eyes right.*) Willie.
(*Pause. Louder.*) Willie. (*Pause. Eyes front.*)
May one still speak of time? (*Pause.*) Say it is
a long time now, Willie, since I saw you.
(*Pause.*) Since I heard you. (*Pause.*) May one?
(*Pause.*) One does. (*Smile.*) The old style!
(*Smile off.*) There is so little one can speak of.
(*Pause.*) One speaks of it all. (*Pause.*) All one
can. (*Pause.*) I used to think . . . (*pause*) . . . I
say I used to think that I would learn to talk
alone. (*Pause.*) By that I mean to myself, the
wilderness. (*Smile.*) But no. (*Smile broader.*)
No no. (*Smile off.*) Ergo you are there.
(*Pause.*) Oh no doubt you are dead, like the
others, no doubt you have died, or gone away
and left me, like the others, it doesn't matter,
you are there. (*Pause. Eyes left.*) The
bag too is there, the same as ever, I can
see it. (*Pause. Eyes right. Louder.*) The
bag is there, Willie, as good as ever, the
one you gave me that day . . . to go to market.
(*Pause. Eyes front.*) That day. (*Pause.*) What
day? (*Pause.*) I used to pray. (*Pause.*) I say
I used to pray. (*Pause.*) Yes, I must confess I
did. (*Smile.*) Not now. (*Smile broader.*) No
no. (*Smile off. Pause.*) Then . . . now . . . what

difficulties here, for the mind. (*Pause.*) To
have been always what I am — and so changed
from what I was. (*Pause.*) I am the one, I say
the one, then the other. (*Pause.*) Now the one,
then the other. (*Pause.*) There is so little one
can say, one says it all. (*Pause.*) All
one can. (*Pause.*) And no truth in it anywhere.
(*Pause.*) My arms. (*Pause.*) My breasts.
(*Pause.*) What arms? (*Pause.*) What breasts?
(*Pause.*) Willie. (*Pause.*) What Willie?
(*Sudden vehement affirmation.*) My Willie!
(*Eyes right, calling.*) Willie! (*Pause. Louder.*)
Willie! (*Pause. Eyes front.*) Ah well, not to
know, not to know for sure, great mercy, all I
ask. (*Pause.*) Ah yes . . . then . . . now . . .
beechen green . . . this . . . Charlie . . . kisses . . .
this . . . all that . . . deep trouble for the mind.
(*Pause.*) But it does not trouble mine. (*Smile.*)
Not now. (*Smile broader.*) No no. (*Smile off.
Long pause. She closes eyes. Bell rings loudly.
She opens eyes. Pause.*) Eyes float up that seem
to close in peace . . . to see . . . in peace. (*Pause.*)
Not mine. (*Smile.*) Not now. (*Smile broader.*)
No no. (*Smile off. Long pause.*) Willie.
(*Pause.*) Do you think the earth has lost its
atmosphere, Willie? (*Pause.*) Do you, Willie?
(*Pause.*) You have no opinion? (*Pause.*) Well

that is like you, you never had any opinion about anything. (*Pause.*) It's understandable. (*Pause.*) Most. (*Pause.*) The earthball. (*Pause.*) I sometimes wonder. (*Pause.*) Perhaps not quite all. (*Pause.*) There always remains something. (*Pause.*) Of everything. (*Pause.*) Some remains. (*Pause.*) If the mind were to go. (*Pause.*) It won't of course. (*Pause.*) Not quite. (*Pause.*) Not mine. (*Smile*) Not now. (*Smile broader.*) No no. (*Smile off. Long pause.*) It might be the eternal cold. (*Pause.*) Everlasting perishing cold. (*Pause.*) Just chance, I take it, happy chance. (*Pause.*) Oh yes, great mercies, great mercies. (*Pause.*) And now? (*Long pause.*) The face. (*Pause.*) The nose. (*She squints down.*) I can see it . . . (*squinting down*) . . . the tip . . . the nostrils . . . breath of life . . . that curve you so admired . . . (*pouts*) . . . a hint of lip . . . (*pouts again*) . . . if I pout them out . . . (*sticks out tongue*) . . . the tongue of course . . . you so admired . . . if I stick it out . . . (*sticks it out again*) . . . the tip . . . (*eyes up*) . . . suspicion of brow . . . eyebrow . . . imagination possibly . . . (*eyes left*) . . . cheek . . . no . . . (*eyes right*) . . . no . . . (*distends cheeks*) . . . even if I puff them out . . . (*eyes left, distends cheeks again*) . . . no . . . no

damask. (*Eyes front.*) That is all. (*Pause.*) The
bag of course . . . (*eyes left*) . . . a little blurred
perhaps . . . but the bag. (*Eyes front. Offhand.*)
The earth of course and sky. (*Eyes right.*)
The sunshade you gave me . . . that day . . .
(*pause*) . . . that day . . . the lake . . . the reeds.
(*Eyes front. Pause.*) What day? (*Pause.*)
What reeds? (*Long pause. Eyes close. Bell
rings loudly. Eyes open. Pause. Eyes right.*)
Brownie of course. (*Pause.*) You remember
Brownie, Willie, I can see him. (*Pause.*)
Brownie is there, Willie, beside me. (*Pause.
Loud.*) Brownie is there, Willie. (*Pause. Eyes
front.*) That is all. (*Pause.*) What would I do
without them? (*Pause.*) What would I do
without them, when words fail? (*Pause.*) Gaze
before me, with compressed lips. (*Long pause
while she does so.*) I cannot. (*Pause.*) Ah yes,
great mercies, great mercies. (*Long pause.
Low.*) Sometimes I hear sounds. (*Listening
expression. Normal voice.*) But not often.
(*Pause.*) They are a boon, sounds are a boon,
they help me . . . through the day. (*Smile*) The
old style! (*Smile off.*) Yes, those are happy
days, when there are sounds. (*Pause.*) When I
hear sounds. (*Pause.*) I used to think . . .
(*pause*) . . . I say I used to think they were in

my head. (*Smile.*) But no. (*Smile broader.*)
No no. (*Smile off.*) That was just logic.
(*Pause.*) Reason. (*Pause.*) I have not lost my
reason. (*Pause.*) Not yet. (*Pause.*)
Not all. (*Pause.*) Some remains. (*Pause.*)
Sounds. (*Pause.*) Like little ... sunderings,
little falls ... apart. (*Pause. Low.*) It's things,
Willie. (*Pause. Normal voice.*) In the bag,
outside the bag. (*Pause.*) Ah yes, things
have their life, that is what I always say,
things have a life. (*Pause.*) Take my
looking-glass, it doesn't need me. (*Pause.*)
The bell. (*Pause.*) It hurts like a knife.
(*Pause.*) A gouge. (*Pause.*) One cannot ignore
it. (*Pause.*) How often ... (*pause*) ... I say
how often I have said, Ignore it, Winnie, ignore
the bell, pay no heed, just sleep and wake, sleep
and wake, as you please, open and close the
eyes, as you please, or in the way you find most
helpful. (*Pause.*) Open and close the eyes,
Winnie, open and close, always that. (*Pause.*)
But no. (*Smile.*) Not now. (*Smile broader.*)
No no. (*Smile off. Pause.*) What now?
(*Pause.*) What now, Willie? (*Long pause.*)
There is my story of course, when all else fails.
(*Pause.*) A life. (*Smile*) A long life. (*Smile
off.*) Beginning in the womb, where life used to

begin, Mildred has memories, she will have
memories, of the womb, before she dies, the
mother's womb. (*Pause.*) She is now four or
five already and has recently been given a big
waxen dolly. (*Pause.*) Fully clothed, complete
outfit. (*Pause.*) Shoes, socks, undies, complete
set, frilly frock, gloves. (*Pause.*) White mesh.
(*Pause.*) A little white straw hat with a chin
elastic. (*Pause.*) Pearly necklet. (*Pause.*) A
little picture-book with legends in real print
to go under her arm when she takes her walk.
(*Pause.*) China blue eyes that open and shut.
(*Pause. Narrative.*) The sun was not well up
when Milly rose, descended the steep . . .
(*pause*) . . . slipped on her nightgown,
descended all alone the steep wooden stairs,
backwards on all fours, though she had been
forbidden to do so, entered the . . . (*pause*) . . .
tiptoed down the silent passage, entered the
nursery and began to undress Dolly. (*Pause.*)
Crept under the table and began to undress
Dolly. (*Pause.*) Scolding her . . . the while.
(*Pause.*) Suddenly a mouse — (*Long pause.*)
Gently, Winnie. (*Long pause. Calling.*)
Willie! (*Pause. Louder.*) Willie! (*Pause. Mild
reproach.*) I sometimes find your attitude a
little strange, Willie, all this time, it is not like

you to be wantonly cruel. (*Pause.*) Strange?
(*Pause.*) No. (*Smile.*) Not here. (*Smile
broader.*) Not now. (*Smile off.*) And yet . . .
(*Suddenly anxious.*) I do hope nothing is amiss.
(*Eyes right, loud.*) Is all well, dear? (*Pause.
Eyes front. To herself.*) God grant he did not
go in head foremost! (*Eyes right, loud.*)
You're not stuck, Willie? (*Pause. Do.*) You're
not jammed, Willie? (*Eyes front, distressed.*)
Perhaps he is crying out for help all this time
and I do not hear him! (*Pause.*) I do of course
hear cries. (*Pause.*) But they are in my head
surely. (*Pause.*) Is it possible that . . . (*Pause.
With finality.*) No no, my head was always
full of cries. (*Pause.*) Faint confused cries.
(*Pause.*) They come. (*Pause.*) Then go.
(*Pause.*) As on a wind. (*Pause.*) That is what
I find so wonderful. (*Pause.*) They cease.
(*Pause.*) Ah yes, great mercies, great
mercies. (*Pause.*) The day is now well
advanced. (*Smile. Smile off.*) And yet it
is perhaps a little soon for my song. (*Pause.*)
To sing too soon is fatal, I always
find. (*Pause.*) On the other hand it is
possible to leave it too late. (*Pause.*) The bell
goes for sleep and one has not sung. (*Pause.*)
The whole day has flown — (*smile, smile off*)

— flown by, quite by, and no song of
any class, kind or description. (*Pause.*)
There is a problem here. (*Pause.*) One
cannot sing . . . just like that, no. (*Pause.*)
It bubbles up, for some unknown reason, the
time is ill chosen, one chokes it back. (*Pause.*)
One says, Now is the time, it is now or never,
and one cannot. (*Pause.*) Simply cannot sing.
(*Pause.*) Not a note. (*Pause.*) Another thing,
Willie, while we are on this subject. (*Pause.*)
The sadness after song. (*Pause.*) Have you
run across that, Willie? (*Pause.*) In the course
of your experience. (*Pause.*) No? (*Pause.*)
Sadness after intimate sexual intercourse one is
familiar with of course. (*Pause.*) You would
concur with Aristotle there, Willie, I fancy.
(*Pause.*) Yes, that one knows and is prepared
to face. (*Pause.*) But after song . . . (*Pause.*) It
does not last of course. (*Pause.*) That is what I
find so wonderful. (*Pause.*) It wears away.
(*Pause.*) What are those exquisite lines?
(*Pause.*) Go forget me why should something
o'er that something shadow fling . . . go forget
me . . . why should sorrow . . . brightly
smile . . . go forget me . . . never hear me . . .
sweetly smile . . . brightly sing . . . (*Pause.
With a sigh.*) One loses one's classics. (*Pause.*)

Oh not all. (*Pause.*) A part. (*Pause.*) A part
remains. (*Pause.*) That is what I find so
wonderful, a part remains, of one's classics, to
help one through the day. (*Pause.*) Oh yes,
many mercies, many mercies. (*Pause.*)
And now? (*Pause.*) And now, Willie?
(*Long pause.*) I call to the eye of the
mind . . . Mr. Shower — or Cooker. (*She
closes her eyes. Bell rings loudly. She opens her
eyes. Pause.*) Hand in hand, in the other hands
bags. (*Pause.*) Getting on . . . in life. (*Pause.*)
No longer young, not yet old. (*Pause.*)
Standing there gaping at me. (*Pause.*) Can't
have been a bad bosom, he says, in its day.
(*Pause.*) Seen worse shoulders, he says, in my
time. (*Pause.*) Does she feel her legs? he says.
(*Pause.*) Is there any life in her legs? he says
(*Pause.*) Has she anything on underneath? he
says. (*Pause.*) Ask her, he says, I'm shy.
(*Pause.*) Ask her what? she says. (*Pause.*) Is
there any life in her legs. (*Pause.*) Has she
anything on underneath. (*Pause.*) Ask her
yourself, she says. (*Pause. With sudden
violence.*) Let go of me for Christ sake and
drop! (*Pause. Do.*) Drop dead! (*Smile.*) But
no. (*Smile broader.*) No no. (*Smile off.*) I
watch them recede. (*Pause.*) Hand in hand —

and the bags. (*Pause.*) Dim. (*Pause.*) Then
gone. (*Pause.*) Last human kind — to stray this
way. (*Pause.*) Up to date. (*Pause.*) And now?
(*Pause. Low.*) Help. (*Pause. Do.*) Help,
Willie. (*Pause. Do.*) No? (*Long pause.
Narrative.*) Suddenly a mouse . . . (*Pause.*)
Suddenly a mouse ran up her little thigh and
Mildred, dropping Dolly in her fright, began
to scream — (*WINNIE gives a sudden
piercing scream*) — and screamed and
screamed — (*WINNIE screams twice*) —
screamed and screamed and screamed
and screamed till all came running, in
their night attire, papa, mamma, Bibby
and . . . old Annie, to see what was the
matter . . . (*pause*) . . . what on earth could
possibly be the matter. (*Pause.*) Too
late. (*Pause.*) Too late. (*Long pause. Just
audible.*) Willie. (*Pause. Normal voice.*) Ah
well, not long now, Winnie, can't be long now,
until the bell for sleep. (*Pause.*) Then you may
close your eyes, then you *must* close your eyes
— and keep them closed. (*Pause.*) Why say
that again? (*Pause.*) I used to think . . .
(*pause.*) . . . I say I used to think there was no
difference between one fraction of a second
and the next. (*Pause.*) I used to say . . .

(*pause*) . . . I say I used to say, Winnie, you are changeless, there is never any difference between one fraction of a second and the next. (*Pause.*) Why bring that up again? (*Pause.*) There is so little one can bring up, one brings up all. (*Pause.*) All one can. (*Pause.*) My neck is hurting me. (*Pause. With sudden violence.*) My neck is hurting me! (*Pause.*) Ah that's better. (*With mild irritation.*) Everything within reason. (*Long pause.*) I can do no more. (*Pause.*) Say no more. (*Pause.*) But I must say more. (*Pause.*) Problem here. (*Pause.*) No, something must move, in the world, I can't any more. (*Pause.*) A zephyr. (*Pause.*) A breath. (*Pause.*) What are those immortal lines? (*Pause.*) It might be the eternal dark. (*Pause.*) Black night without end. (*Pause.*) Just chance, I take it, happy chance. (*Pause.*) Oh yes, abounding mercies. (*Long pause.*) And now? (*Pause.*) And now, Willie? (*Long pause.*) That day. (*Pause.*) The pink fizz. (*Pause.*) The flute glasses. (*Pause.*) The last guest gone. (*Pause.*) The last bumper with the bodies nearly touching. (*Pause.*) The look. (*Long pause.*) What day? (*Long pause.*) What look? (*Long pause.*) I hear cries. (*Pause.*) Sing. (*Pause.*) Sing your old song, Winnie.

Long pause. Suddenly alert expression. Eyes switch right. WILLIE's head appears to her right round corner of mound. He is on all fours, dressed to kill — top hat, morning coat, striped trousers, etc., white gloves in hand. Very long bushy white Battle of Britain moustache. He halts, gazes front, smooths moustache. He emerges completely from behind mound, turns to his left, halts, looks up at WINNIE. He advances on all fours towards centre, halts, turns head front, gazes front, strokes moustache, straightens tie, adjusts hat, advances a little further, halts, takes off hat and looks up at WINNIE. He is now not far from centre and within her field of vision. Unable to sustain effort of looking up he sinks head to ground.

WINNIE   (*mondaine*). Well this is an unexpected pleasure! (*Pause.*) Reminds me of the day you came whining for my hand. (*Pause.*) I worship you, Winnie, be mine. (*He looks up.*) Life a mockery without Win. (*She goes off into a giggle.*) What a get up, you do look a sight! (*Giggles.*) Where are the flowers? (*Pause.*) That smile today. (*WILLIE sinks head.*) What's that on your neck, an anthrax?

(*Pause.*) Want to watch that, Willie, before it gets a hold on you. (*Pause.*) Where were you all this time? (*Pause.*) What were you doing all this time? (*Pause.*) Changing? (*Pause.*) Did you not hear me screaming for you? (*Pause.*) Did you get stuck in your hole? (*Pause. He looks up.*) That's right, Willie, look at me. (*Pause.*) Feast your old eyes, Willie. (*Pause.*) Does anything remain? (*Pause.*) Any remains? (*Pause.*) No? (*Pause.*) I haven't been able to look after it, you know. (*He sinks his head.*) You are still recognizable, in a way. (*Pause.*) Are you thinking of coming to live this side now . . . for a bit maybe? (*Pause.*) No? (*Pause.*) Just a brief call? (*Pause.*) Have you gone deaf, Willie? (*Pause.*) Dumb? (*Pause.*) Oh I know you were never one to talk, I worship you Winnie be mine and then nothing from that day forth only titbits from Reynolds' News. (*Eyes front. Pause.*) Ah well, what matter, that's what I always say, it will have been a happy day, after all, another happy day. (*Pause.*) Not long now, Winnie. (*Pause.*) I hear cries. (*Pause.*) Do you ever hear cries, Willie? (*Pause.*) No? (*Eyes back on WILLIE.*) Willie. (*Pause.*) Look at me again, Willie. (*Pause.*) Once more, Willie. (*He looks*

up. Happily.) Ah! (*Pause. Shocked.*) What
ails you, Willie, I never saw such an expression!
(*Pause.*) Put on your hat, dear, it's the sun,
don't stand on ceremony, I won't mind. (*He
drops hat and gloves and starts to crawl up
mound towards her. Gleeful.*) Oh I say, this
is terrific! (*He halts, clinging to mound with
one hand, reaching up with the other.*) Come
on, dear, put a bit of jizz into it, I'll cheer you
on. (*Pause.*) Is it me you're after, Willie . . .
or is it something else? (*Pause.*) Do you want
to touch my face . . . again? (*Pause.*) Is it a kiss
you're after, Willie . . . or is it something else?
(*Pause.*) There was a time when I could have
given you a hand. (*Pause.*) And then a time
before that again when I did give you a hand.
(*Pause.*) You were always in dire need of a
hand, Willie. (*He slithers back to foot of
mound and lies with face to ground.*) Brrum!
(*Pause. He rises to hands and knees, raises his
face towards her.*) Have another go, Willie, I'll
cheer you on. (*Pause.*) Don't look at me like
that! (*Pause. Vehement.*) Don't look at me
like that! (*Pause. Low.*) Have you gone off
your head, Willie? (*Pause. Do.*) Out of your
poor old wits, Willie?

Pause.

WILLIE   (*just audible*). Win.

*Pause. WINNIE's eyes front. Happy
expression appears, grows.*

WINNIE   Win! (*Pause.*) Oh this *is* a happy day, this will
have been another happy day! (*Pause.*) After
all. (*Pause.*) So far.

*Pause. She hums tentatively beginning of song,
then sings softly, musical-box tune.*

> Though I say not
> What I may not
> Let you hear,
> Yet the swaying
> Dance is saying,
> Love me dear!
> Every touch of fingers
> Tells me what I know,
> Says for you,
> It's true, it's true,
> You love me so!

*Pause. Happy expression off. She closes her
eyes. Bell rings loudly. She opens her eyes. She
smiles, gazing front. She turns her eyes, smiling,
to WILLIE, still on his hands and knees
looking up at her. Smile off. They look at each
other. Long pause.*

CURTAIN